Contents

Note to adults:

There are many varieties of catnip. Cats are particularly attracted to *Nepeta cataria*, and this is the plant you should use. *Nepeta x faassenii* is an ornamental plant and is less attractive to cats.

What is catnip?

Catnip is a garden plant. It is also called catmint. Catnip is very useful. Its leaves can be used to make tea. It is also used as a medicine for colds and tummy upsets.

There are many types of catnip, but the type cats like best is called *Nepeta cataria.*

This cat is rolling on young catnip plants.

Cats love catnip! They like its smell. They rub against the plant and bite its leaves. Dried catnip is put into toys for cats to play with. It is not only pet cats that like catnip. Lions, tigers, and other big cats like it, too.

Catnip close up

Catnip is a bushy plant with grey-green leaves. The leaves are oval, have **serrated** edges, and end in a point. The **stems** and leaves are covered in little hairs.

serrated edges

stem

This bee is drinking nectar from a catnip flower. ▶

Catnip plants grow to about 60 centimetres high. They make flowers in the summer. The flowers can be white or purple. Bees love to crawl into the flowers to feed on their **nectar**.

Why do cats like catnip?

Catnip plants make a special type of **oil**. When cats smell the oil, it makes them think of other cats. They become very playful.

Cats love the smell of catnip.

This cat has found some catnip plants!

Cats bite catnip leaves and roll around in the plants. They do this to crush the plants. It makes the plants **release** more of their oil. Cats go crazy for catnip!

Catnip and your cat

Catnip can be used as a treat for a cat. Pet shops sell sprays that smell of catnip. It can be sprayed on to a cat's **scratching post**. The cat will love to scratch and nibble at the post.

scratching post

A little cushion filled with dried catnip makes a great toy for a cat to play with.

Catnip leaves can be dried and put into toys for cats. Cats love to play with catnip toys. They nibble at them and carry them around the house. You can make a catnip toy for a cat you know.

Grow your own catnip

It is easy to grow catnip. The plants will grow almost anywhere. They need very little looking after, and very little water.

This catnip is growing in a flower bed.

catnip

baby catnip plant

catnip seeds

CATMINT

ENJOYED BY CATS EVERYWHERE!

You can buy packets of catnip **seeds** and baby catnip plants at a garden centre. Once you have catnip growing in your garden, it will come up again year after year.

Where to grow catnip

Catnip grows outside. You can grow it in a garden **flower border**, or in a large plant pot. It likes to grow in a sunny place. It does not like to be in the **shade**.

It does not take long for baby catnip plants to grow. ▶

14

If you don't want catnip to spread as much as this, you can grow it in a pot instead.

Catnip spreads. Each year it makes new plants, which cover more and more ground. Choose a growing area you don't mind it spreading over.

Grow catnip from seed

In early spring, clear the growing area of weeds. Then, make a **seed bed** to **sow** your catnip **seeds** in. Loosen the soil with a garden fork. Break up any lumps. Rake it over to remove stones.

Pull a rake across the soil to catch stones and move them out of the way.

seed bed

Sow catnip seeds by scattering them across the surface of the soil.

Pour a few seeds into your hand. Take little pinches of the seeds and **scatter** them across the seed bed. Use a rake to mix the seeds into the soil. Sprinkle water over the soil with a watering can.

17

Watering the seed bed

Keep the **seed bed** watered, especially in dry weather. Try not to let the soil dry out or the **seeds** will not grow. If it has been raining, the rain will have done the watering for you.

Use a **watering rose** to sprinkle water gently over the seed bed.

watering rose

Seedlings have tiny leaves and **stems**.

After two or three weeks, look out for the tiny leaves of the first **seedlings**. It is often easier to spot them after the soil has been watered.

Too many plants!

If all the **seeds** grow, you will have too many plants. The growing area will become overcrowded. The plants won't like it. You need to **thin** them out when they are little.

These catnip plants are growing too close to each other.

Catnip plants need room to grow.

When the plants are about 10 centimetres high, decide which ones to keep. They should be about 30 centimetres apart. Pull up the ones you don't want and put them on to your **compost heap**.

Stay away cats!

Cats will soon find out that you are growing catnip. They will sneak into your garden, nibble the plants and roll around in them. This is fun to watch.

Cats can often smell catnip from far away.

Cats can make a mess of your plants. If you cover the plants with garden **netting**, cats will stay away from the plants.

Harvesting your catnip

By mid-summer, catnip is fully grown. It is time to **harvest** the leaves for your cat toy. Ask an adult to cut the **stems** about 20 centimetres from the ground. You will need lots of leaves, so cut lots of stems.

Ask an adult to cut the catnip for you.

Catnip leaves will turn darker green as they dry.

Pull the leaves off the stems and put them on a tray. Put the tray on a windowsill and leave it for a few days so that the leaves can dry out.

25

Crush the leaves

When the leaves are completely dry, they will be **brittle**. Put them into a big bowl. Crunch them up and rub them together with your hands.

Dried catnip leaves look like this. ▶

Rub the leaves with your hands. This breaks them into tiny pieces.

Breaking the leaves into tiny pieces helps to **release** the smell of the catnip.

Make a catnip toy

Now you can use your catnip to make a ball for a cat to play with. Please ask an adult to help you with this activity.

You will need:
  an old sock,
  scissors,
  a needle,
  thread,
  dried catnip leaves,
  and a piece of string about 1 metre long.

1. Cut the toe end off the sock. It should be about 10 centimetres long.
2. Fill the toe with the crushed catnip leaves until it starts to become round, like a ball.
3. Ask an adult to sew the open end of the sock to close it.
4. Tie the string onto the sock. Your cat toy is finished!

Glossary

brittle something which breaks or snaps easily

compost heap a pile of old plants, grass cuttings, and leaves which are left to rot down

flower border the part of a garden where flowers grow

harvest to gather fruit and vegetables when they are ready to pick or dig up

nectar a sugary liquid made by plants

netting a plastic net with holes in it

oil a type of liquid

release to let go of something

scatter to spread seeds across an area by throwing them

scratching post a post for a cat to scratch at

seed the part of a plant that grows into a new plant

seed bed an area of fine soil where seeds are sown

seedling a baby plant

serrated having a notched or jagged edge

shade a darker area of the garden, where trees or buildings cast shadows

sow to plant a seed

stem the main branch or trunk of a plant

thin to remove unwanted plants so that the rest of the plants have more space

watering rose a sprinkler on the end of a watering can

Find out more

Books to read

Grow It, Eat It, D. K. Publishing (Dorling Kindersley, 2008)

Ready, Steady, Grow!, Royal Horticultural Society (Dorling Kindersley, 2010)

Websites

www.bluebirdgardens.com/?realm=Cats&page=Catnip
Find out lots of information about catnip and how to make catnip toys on this website.

www.kiddiegardens.com
This site will give you lots of ideas on how to grow plants that you can use to make things.

www.thekidsgarden.co.uk
Discover more gardening ideas and activities on this website.

Index